Manage Your Way to Millions

---

7 Steps. Take Control. Build Wealth.
No Excuses.

Eric Bowie (Smart Money Bro®)

MANAGE YOUR WAY TO MILLIONS

ISBN 979-8-218-85294-8 (paperback)

ISBN 979-8-218-85295-5 (hardback)

www.smartmoneybro.com

Table of Contents

Introduction

Have you ever felt like no matter how hard you work or how much you earn, financial freedom still seems just out of reach?

I've been there. For years, I watched good money slip through my fingers like sand, wondering why some people build wealth on modest incomes while others stay broke making six figures. What I discovered changed everything, and it wasn't about making more money.

This book delivers a proven, systematic approach to building real wealth that works at any income level, not by chasing bigger paychecks, but by mastering the one skill most financial experts overlook: proper management of whatever money you already have.

You can achieve financial freedom without a six-figure salary, without an inheritance or winning the lottery, or without already knowing the secrets of investing. My approach flips conventional wisdom on its head by focusing first on mastering the money you already have before chasing more income. When you implement this system, you'll discover that wealth-building isn't about what you make—it's about your behavior with whatever you make.

This book is for:

1) Working adults who feel stuck in the paycheck-to-paycheck cycle despite making decent money

2) People who want to eliminate debt permanently and build lasting wealth regardless of their current income level

3) Parents and future parents who want to create financial security for themselves while establishing a legacy that can transform their family for generations.

I discovered this system by accident when I was struggling with my own finances despite earning a decent income. Before I was 30 years old, I had no written plan for my money and watched as thousands of dollars slipped through my fingers each year. It wasn't until I started writing everything down and creating a personalized management system that I began to build real wealth. What started as my personal solution evolved over decades into a comprehensive approach that has helped countless people transform their financial lives regardless of their starting point.

The financial reality most Americans face is staggering. According to the Federal Reserve, 36% of Americans would struggle to cover a $400 emergency expense without borrowing money or selling something.

Even more troubling, nearly 78% of full-time workers live paycheck to paycheck despite the median household income exceeding $70,000.

These aren't just statistics. They represent millions of hardworking people who feel trapped despite doing "everything right" according to conventional wisdom.

Traditional financial advice fails because it often focuses on complex investment strategies that require significant starting capital, or it emphasizes increasing income without addressing the fundamental management issues that cause most financial problems.

People spend years trying to follow complicated budgeting systems that demand hours each week to maintain, or they waste time pursuing minimal returns while their day-to-day finances remain in chaos. The frustration builds as you watch your hard-earned money disappear despite your best efforts, leaving you wondering if financial security is even possible for "regular people" without specialized knowledge or extraordinary income. This approach is like trying to fill a leaky bucket by adding more water instead of fixing the holes.

But here's the kicker...

Proper money management has never been more critical than it is right now. Look around you. With economic uncertainty, rising costs, and so many financial products competing for your attention, taking complete control of your finances isn't just nice to have—it's essential for survival and building wealth in today's world.

The good news?

You don't need to wait for the "perfect time" or for your income to increase. You can start implementing this system today with whatever you currently earn.

Whatever you mismanage, you lose. That's a truth I've seen play out countless times. Your behavior, not your income, will determine your wealth. This system isn't about restricting your life. It's about taking the position of manager over your money so it becomes your employee, not your boss. You gotta manage at a new level to get to a new level, and that's exactly what this book will show you how to do.

My financial life was like trying to carry water in cupped hands. It just kept leaking through my fingers no matter how much came in. But since implementing this system, I've eliminated over $70,000 in student loan debt that had ballooned from an initial $50,000, built a substantial emergency fund of $30,000 that gives me complete peace of mind, and maintained a credit score of near 800 despite keeping my credit frozen for nearly 13 years as a security measure. This system works in real life, not just on paper.

In the first chapter, we'll begin with the most crucial element of financial success: understanding why management matters more than income. You'll discover how to develop the right mindset and organizational approach that makes everything else possible. This foundation isn't complicated, but it's the missing piece that explains why so many people struggle financially despite knowing what they "should" do.

By starting with proper management, you'll position yourself to build wealth in a way that feels natural rather than forced, creating momentum that carries you through each subsequent step of the system.

Chapter 1
Money Management: Your Path to Financial Freedom

The Foundation of Financial Freedom

Have you ever watched someone crash and burn financially despite making six figures? Or wondered how your coworker affords vacations on the same salary that barely covers your bills?

I've seen doctors making $300,000 a year file for bankruptcy. I've watched janitors with modest incomes build impressive investment portfolios. The difference wasn't their paychecks. It was how they managed what landed in their accounts.

Here's a truth that might be hard to swallow: Your behavior, not your income, will determine your wealth. Financial freedom isn't about what you make. It's about what you do with what you make.

I learned this lesson the hard way. Before my 30th birthday, I was making decent money but had little to show for it. It wasn't until I developed a management system that my financial situation began to transform.

Financial management is the foundation everything else is built upon. Without it, no amount of income can save you from financial struggles. With it, even modest earnings can grow into significant wealth. Before we dive into budgeting techniques or investment strategies, we need to understand why management itself holds the key to your financial future.

What Is Financial Management?

Financial management is simply getting organized with your money. It means creating a clear plan on paper for how you'll handle your finances. At its core, financial management is a personalized system that helps you take control of your resources—your income, assets, and financial tools—and use them effectively. It's about creating a structure that works specifically for your situation to help you make the most of what you have.

It's a process tailored specifically to you that fits your personal financial situation, your geography, and your goals. Because personal finance is "personal", financial management is about taking your resources and developing a process where you utilize those resources to best suit you, your family, and your future.

Think of it as creating a roadmap for your money. Without this map, you're just wandering, hoping to stumble upon financial success. With it, every dollar has a purpose and a direction.

Now, understanding what good financial management looks like is one thing, but recognizing why so many people struggle to implement it is equally important. By identifying these challenges, we can better prepare ourselves to overcome them.

Why People Struggle with Money Management

People struggle with managing their finances for so many different reasons, and I've seen these challenges play out repeatedly in my years of financial coaching. Understanding these roadblocks isn't just helpful, it's essential if you want to overcome them and create lasting financial change. Let's look at some of the biggest obstacles I've observed that keep people trapped in poor money management habits.

Self-Management Challenges

Many people have a hard time managing themselves, so naturally, they struggle to manage their money. If you can't tell yourself "no" when it comes to personal desires, how can you expect to control your financial decisions?

Financial management requires self-discipline. You need to be able to delay gratification and make decisions based on long-term goals rather than immediate wants. Unfortunately, many of us weren't taught these skills growing up.

Lack of Financial Education

Money management isn't commonly taught in schools. Most people enter adulthood without understanding basic financial principles. They're expected to somehow know how to budget, save, invest, and plan for the future without ever receiving formal instruction on these topics.

This knowledge gap creates a significant disadvantage, especially for those from communities where financial literacy isn't emphasized. Without proper education, people often repeat the financial mistakes they've seen modeled around them.

The Social Media Effect

One of the most powerful challenges in today's world is social media's influence on our financial decisions. Every day, billions of people across the globe log onto social media platforms and see a highlight reel of everyone's greatest moments.

It's like watching ESPN highlights of a basketball game. They're going to show you LeBron James dunking the ball, but they're not going to show you Bill Jones, who had 25 rebounds. They show you the highlights, so you think the whole game was just LeBron making spectacular plays.

This tricks your brain into thinking that's how everyone is living. You don't see the financial sacrifices, the budgeting, the saying "no" to purchases, or the years of consistent saving that made those highlights possible. Instead, you see the vacation, the new car, the designer clothes, and you think that's normal everyday life.

This distorted perception directly impacts how people approach money management. When you consume these highlights, you begin to think, "I want to manage my money like the highlights." It's like walking into a gym and the first thing you do is try to dunk. You can't pass, you can't dribble, you can't play defense, but all you're thinking about is dunking. We've all seen that person who's an awesome dunker but can't actually play basketball.

The same happens with money. People mimic the lifestyle they see in social media highlights while neglecting the fundamentals of financial management that happen behind the scenes.

Understanding these challenges is crucial, but identifying problems is only helpful if we follow through with solutions. Let's turn our attention now to the practical steps you can take to overcome these obstacles and become intentional about your financial management.

Why How You Manage Money Trumps How Much You Make

Many people fall into the trap of thinking, "If I just made more money, all my financial problems would disappear." I hear this all the time from folks making $50,000 who believe their money troubles would vanish if they could just earn $150,000 or $500,000. The reality is much different though. If you can't effectively manage the money you have now, more income will only amplify your management problems, not solve them.

Life's Limited Timeline

We're all here for a relatively short time. I'm 55. You might be in your 30s or 40s. The truth is, none of us know exactly how long we have. Unlike the ancient Egyptians who believed in being buried with their possessions, we enter this world with nothing and leave with nothing. Everything we receive during our time here is temporary, it's entrusted to us for a season. This perspective should shape how we approach money management and make us wise stewards over our money. Since everything flows through our hands for a limited time, our job is to manage it well while we have it.

Whatever You Mismanage, You Lose

Everything that flows through our hands—whether it's money, time, relationships, or possessions—needs to be managed while we have it. Money is currency, and like water, it flows to you and through you. What matters is what you do with it when you have it.

I grew up without much money. In fact, I was very poor as a child. But that experience taught me something invaluable. I learned at a very young age to take very good care of what little I did have. That early lesson in stewardship laid the foundation for how I approach money management today, even when handling much larger sums. The principles remain the same whether you're managing $100 or $100,000.

One misconception I want to address is this idea that "poor equals raggedy" or that limited finances must translate to carelessness. Nowadays, many people think being poor means looking a certain way or engaging in certain behaviors. But I grew up in a time when I was taught that just because you're poor doesn't mean you have to look a certain way or act a certain way. You can still maintain what you have with care and dignity. Financial management isn't just for the wealthy. It's perhaps even more critical when resources are limited.

This principle applies regardless of income level. If you take good care of the little things, you make room for bigger things. If you have an old car and you don't maintain it, what makes you think you're positioning yourself to receive a better one? The principle is simple: if you take good care of what you have, good things will be added to you.

The Parable of the Talents

This reminds me of the parable of the talents in the Bible, which has deeply shaped my view of money management.

In this parable, a master gives his servants different amounts of money (talents) to manage while he's away. The ones who invested and grew their talents were rewarded, while the one who buried his talent and did nothing with it was punished. This biblical principle guides my approach to finances. It's a reminder that you have to do something productive with what you've been given, not just let it sit and collect dust. You have to manage it well so you can grow it. This isn't just good financial advice; it's a spiritual principle of stewardship that applies to everything in our lives.

Whatever you mismanage, you lose. It's a core principle: take good care of what you have so that you'll be in position to have more and be trustworthy with more. If you can't be trusted with a dollar, can you really be trusted with two dollars or even one million dollars? Probably not.

This principle explains why simply increasing your income rarely solves financial problems, and can sometimes make them worse.

When More Money Makes Things Worse

Adding more income to poor money management is like taking an alcoholic and placing them in the middle of a liquor store. If they couldn't manage one beer a week, how do you expect them to handle themselves when they're around 3,000 beers?

You never want to pour more money on top of poor money behaviors. First, fix the management, then seek ways to increase your income.

Many people focus on learning about investing, real estate, and other wealth-building strategies while completely overlooking management. They want to jump straight to advanced wealth techniques without mastering the fundamentals. But here's the truth: none of those wealth-building strategies will work effectively without proper management as the foundation. It's like trying to build a skyscraper without first creating a solid foundation. Eventually, everything will collapse.

How Discipline Drives Management

Management is fundamentally about discipline, and discipline is at the core of how we manage ourselves. Life itself requires discipline. Everything is available to you, but not everything is beneficial for you. You must have the discipline to make wise choices.

If someone asked, "What is being disciplined with money?" the answer would be "Managing money well." Just as discipline is at the core of living our everyday lives, management is at the core of taking care of your money.

There are plenty of high-income earners who don't have much wealth because they're poor managers. They make a lot of money but spend just as much or more. Remember, whatever you mismanage—whether it's relationships, education, or money—you'll eventually lose because you're not being disciplined with it.

Becoming Intentional About Financial Management

Understanding why management matters is just the beginning. The real challenge and the real opportunity lies in putting these principles into practice in your daily financial life. I've found that people who successfully transform their financial situations follow a specific set of steps that anyone can implement, regardless of income level or current financial status. Here's where you need to start if you want to master the art of financial management.

1. Respect the Importance of Management

The first step to becoming intentional is understanding and respecting the place that management has in your financial life. If you don't believe management is important, you won't give it the attention it deserves. Recognize that without proper management, no other financial strategy will work effectively.

2. Develop Management Habits

Thinking about management is one thing, but doing it is something different. Start developing habits around good management:

- **Document your financial plans:** Write down your financial goals, strategies, and timelines.

- **Create financial mission and vision statements:** What do you want your relationship with money to look like? Where do you want to be financially in 5, 10, or 20 years?

- **Set specific, measurable goals:** Don't just say "I want to save more." Set a specific target: "I will save $500 per month toward my emergency fund until I reach $10,000."

- **Outline action steps:** For each goal, list the specific actions you'll take to achieve it.

3. Take Financial Management Seriously

Approach your financial management with the same seriousness you would approach studying for a crucial final exam. If you knew that passing one class was the difference between receiving your four-year degree or not, you would take that class seriously. You would write things down, study consistently, and revisit your notes regularly.

Apply this same level of dedication to managing your money. This isn't something you do once and forget about. It's an ongoing process that requires regular attention and refinement.

4. Put It on Paper

Before I was 30 years old, I really didn't have a written plan for my money. I never wrote anything down, other than my monthly budget. It wasn't until I started really writing things down and getting organized with my money that I began to build wealth.

I've always been a paper person. If I look on my desk right now, you'd see stacks of notebooks—different colors, different sizes, some going back years. These aren't just for show. These notebooks are where I record everything about my finances. Every dollar coming in, every dollar going out. Budget plans, debt payoff strategies, savings goals. It's all there in black and white. I keep all these things written down because I don't like relying on my memory, especially when it comes to something as important as my money. These notebooks tell the story of my financial journey, and they've been one of my most powerful tools for building wealth.

Think about the things in your life that you take seriously, your career, your health, your relationships. You probably have systems in place for those important areas. You schedule doctor appointments, you prepare for work presentations, you plan special occasions with loved ones. Your financial life deserves that same level of intentional attention. When you commit to putting your financial plans on paper and reviewing them regularly, you create a powerful system that can transform your relationship with money.

Why Everything Else Fails Without Management

Management is the cornerstone of everything you do in terms of personal finances. If you don't get the management right, nothing else is going to work—not the investing, not the real estate, not the wealth-building strategies. Nothing works in our financial lives without proper management.

Financial management doesn't just happen. Organizational skills aren't going to knock on your door and introduce themselves. You have to be proactive. You have to be intentional. You have to do the work.

You can make as much money as you want, but if you don't know how to manage it, it won't matter. Management requires intention, and without intention, financial success will always remain just out of reach.

Now that we understand why management is the foundation of financial success, we need a practical system to implement these principles. In the next chapter, we'll explore budgeting—the primary tool that transforms these management concepts into daily actions. You'll learn how to create a system that gives you complete control over your money and establishes the framework for building lasting wealth.

Chapter 2

Command and Control: Mastering Your Money Through Budgeting

Taking Command of Your Financial Life

Ever felt completely out of control with your money? Like you're constantly reacting to financial emergencies rather than directing where your dollars go?

You're not alone.

Most people experience this feeling at some point—watching money flow in and out without truly understanding where it's going or having the power to guide it.

Now that we've established management as the foundation of financial success, we need to explore the primary tool that enables that management: the budget. But this isn't just about creating a spreadsheet or using an app. It's about fundamentally shifting your relationship with money from reaction to intentional direction. So what does it really mean to control your money instead of letting it control you? It starts with understanding the flow of every dollar in your financial life.

What Real Financial Control Looks Like

Controlling your money means understanding both where it's coming from and where it's going. In other words, you gotta know the flow.

At its core, this means being "in the know" about your financial situation, not working with approximations or guesses, but specific numbers. You need to know exactly how much is coming in and precisely where each dollar is going out.

Why does this matter so much?

Because control equals power, and power is exactly what you want to have over your money. When you lack this power, it becomes dangerously easy to slip into undisciplined behaviors, allowing your money to control you instead.

Think about how you feel in any situation where you lack control. If you're walking down the street and suddenly hear gunshots and see people running, that out-of-control feeling triggers immediate stress, anxiety, and fear. Your adrenaline spikes, and negative emotions take over. The same psychological response happens with finances. When you don't feel in control of your money, it creates emotional turbulence that affects your entire life.

Conversely, when you have control, you experience peace. Imagine knowing that you have $5,000 coming in this month, $4,000 going out, and you've planned for every dollar. You've got it all mapped out on paper. You know exactly where everything's going. Whew. That feels kind of good, right? You can think, "This is cool. Okay, I can do this, I can watch my show, I can do whatever I gotta do." That settled feeling allows you to relax, breathe easier, and focus your energy on other aspects of life because you're not constantly worried about your money situation.

This is why controlling your money matters. It's not just about dollars and cents, but about creating emotional stability. Control is both power and peace.

Becoming the Boss of Your Money

One of the most powerful ways to think about your relationship with money is to see yourself as the manager and your money as the employee. As a manager, you direct, guide, and oversee your employees. You assign tasks, monitor performance, and ensure everything runs according to plan.

When you take on this managerial role with your finances, you position yourself as the authority figure. Money doesn't tell you what to do, you tell it what to do. This mental shift transforms your financial life because it reminds you that YOU are in control, not your impulses, not your bank account balance, and certainly not consumer culture.

Just as a good manager needs systems to effectively oversee employees, you need a system to manage your money. This is where budgeting comes in. A budget is the primary management tool that gives you the authority to direct your money effectively. Without it, you're like a manager trying to run a department without any processes or accountability systems in place.

Why Budgeting Is Non-Negotiable

Budgeting serves as the cornerstone of financial control because it transforms vague intentions into concrete actions. Without a budget, your financial goals remain mere wishes. With a budget, you create a roadmap that guides every dollar toward your desired destination. This management tool works in several powerful ways, starting with its role as your personal accountability partner.

1. Your Accountability Partner

Most of us manage our money in isolation. We keep our financial decisions in a private "box" that may include our spouse or partner but rarely extends beyond that. Since you likely don't have someone looking over your shoulder to help you stay accountable with every financial decision, you need a system that performs this function.

A budget becomes your accountability partner on paper. It's a record of what you promised yourself you would do with your money, and it holds you responsible for those commitments. When you write down, "I will spend $400 on groceries this month," that statement becomes a standard against which you can measure your actual behavior.

Beyond accountability, your budget serves another crucial function: it acts as a mirror that reveals your true habits.

2. A Mirror That Reveals Your True Habits

The budget serves as a mirror, revealing your true financial habits in black and white. For many people, seeing their spending patterns documented this way is genuinely shocking. It often marks the first time they truly confront the reality of where their money actually goes.

When I work one-on-one with clients, I always share screens to review their budget and net worth statements. For many, it's the first time they've ever seen their financial reality laid out so clearly. The reaction is often one of two extremes: either "Wow, I didn't know I had that much money!" or "Wow, I'm in worse shape than I thought."

These revelations don't happen until you see your financial life on paper. Your budget provides this mirror every single month.

Once you can see your habits clearly, your budget takes on yet another important role: it becomes the guardrails that prevent financial disaster.

3. Guardrails That Prevent Financial Disaster

Think of your budget as the guardrails on a highway. When you're driving at high speeds, guardrails aren't there to restrict your freedom. They're there to keep you from plunging off the road into dangerous territory.

Your budget works the same way. It's not a constraint designed to make your life less enjoyable. It's a protective system that prevents you from falling into the dangerous territory of financial instability. These guardrails provide structure and discipline that keep you safely on track toward your financial goals.

These protective guardrails work because your budget creates something essential: a permanent record of your financial journey.

4. A Permanent Record of Your Financial Journey

Your budget does more than guide today's spending. It creates a lasting record of your financial decisions. Think about how important documenting and keeping records of important events is in other areas. For example, we read the Bible today because those teachings were carefully recorded centuries ago. Similarly, recording your financial journey provides invaluable insights over time.

Would you trust an accountant who didn't keep records? Of course not. We inherently understand the value of documentation when it comes to important matters. Your personal finances deserve the same level of record-keeping.

A budget serves as the official record of your financial life—documenting what comes in and what goes out. This historical record becomes invaluable over time, allowing you to track progress, identify patterns, and make better decisions based on actual data rather than memory or impression.

This record-keeping isn't just practical. It's fundamentally empowering. This entire financial management process is about taking back your power and exercising proper dominion over the resources you've been given.

5. An Empowering Tool That Gives You Dominion

We're supposed to take dominion over the resources entrusted to us. Dominion, at its core, means exercising proper control and stewardship. When you write down your budget, you're essentially declaring, "I'm taking dominion over my finances by tracking everything that comes in and goes out of my life."

When you create a budget, you're positioning yourself in the middle of the river of your life, controlling the currency—the flow coming in and the flow going out. You're no longer passively watching money wash away; you're actively directing its course.

The Power of a Zero-Based Budget

While there are many budgeting methods available, the zero-based budget stands out as particularly effective for taking complete control of your finances.

What Is a Zero-Based Budget?

A zero-based budget is a method where you allocate every single dollar of your income to a specific purpose before you spend it. The concept originated in the 1970s as a business term, focusing on tracking every penny to maximize profit. In the last 20 years, the personal finance community has adopted this approach because it provides maximum control over personal finances.

The term "zero-based" comes from the principle that after you've assigned all your income to various categories (expenses, savings, debt payments, etc.), the difference between your income and allocations should be zero. Every dollar has a job.

Why Zero-Based Budgeting Works

What makes zero-based budgeting so effective is its emphasis on complete control. Rather than roughly planning for most of your expenses while leaving some money unaccounted for, you make a plan for every single dollar.

It accentuates the discipline piece. It allows you to be ultra, ultra particular and specific. In other words, it's the ability to take total control, not just control.

If you bring home $3,001.02 this month, you're not just planning for $3,000—you're planning for the entire $3,001.02. This level of detail might seem excessive, but it serves an important purpose: it develops the habit of conscious, intentional money management down to the penny.

Think of it as being "nitpicky with every single penny." You're going overboard with the habit so that the habit gets deeply ingrained.

What Zero-Based Budgeting Looks Like in Practice

Let's look at what this means in real life. A zero-based budget breaks down every dollar into specific categories like:

- **Housing:** $1,500 (rent/mortgage, insurance, property taxes)
- **Utilities:** $350 (electric, water, gas, internet)
- **Transportation:** $400 (car payment, insurance, gas, maintenance)
- **Food:** $600 (groceries $500, dining out $100)
- **Debt Repayment:** $300 (student loans, credit cards)

- **Savings:** $400 (emergency fund, retirement)
- **Personal:** $200 (clothing, haircuts, gym)
- **Entertainment:** $150 (streaming services, movies, hobbies)
- **Miscellaneous:** $100 (unexpected expenses)

For someone with a monthly income of $4,000, their total allocated spending would equal exactly $4,000. Notice how specific each category is. It's not just vague labels like "bills" or "spending money," but every single dollar is given a specific job to do. This level of detail might seem like overkill at first, but it's exactly what creates the control and clarity that leads to financial peace.

Building Flexibility Into Your Zero-Based Budget

While zero-based budgeting is precise, it doesn't have to be rigid. You can build flexibility into the system while still maintaining complete control.

For example, you might allocate $200 to a "miscellaneous" category each month. This is still spending every dollar on paper, but it gives you some leeway to handle unexpected expenses or small indulgences without derailing your entire plan.

The key is that even your "flexible" spending is planned. You've made a conscious decision about how much flexibility you need, rather than letting unplanned spending happen by default.

Why People Fail at Budgeting

Despite the clear benefits of budgeting, many people either never start or fail to stick with it long-term. Understanding these common pitfalls can help you avoid them:

1. Laziness and Lack of Follow-Through

Let's keep it 100: the number one reason people fail at budgeting is simple laziness. When you start something and don't finish it, that's just having a quitter's mentality.

Creating a budget isn't difficult. The real work lies in the discipline to maintain it consistently, especially when you don't feel like it. Many people get excited about budgeting at first but lose steam when it requires ongoing attention, preferring activities with more immediate rewards.

While laziness might be the primary culprit, there's another challenge deeply rooted in our modern culture: the inability to delay gratification.

2. Inability to Delay Gratification

We live in a world of instant results. When you post on social media, you get likes within minutes. When you order online, products arrive the next day. But budgeting doesn't provide this immediate gratification.

The benefits of budgeting often take months or years to fully materialize. You're developing habits that will serve you well in the long term, but you may not see dramatic results in the first few weeks. Without the ability to delay gratification and trust in the process, many people abandon their budgets when they don't see immediate payoff.

Even if you can overcome the need for instant results, budgeting still requires something more fundamental: a clear vision of what you're working toward.

3. Lack of Vision and Goals

One of the problems with this whole thing is that people don't have vision. And if you don't have vision, then you don't have the why to do it today because you can't see down the road.

Many people budget without a clear purpose. They're going through the motions without understanding why budgeting matters for their future. Without specific financial goals—whether it's building an emergency fund, paying off debt, or saving for a home—budgeting can feel like pointless restriction.

Your budget needs to be connected to your why. What are you working toward? What future are you building?

Without this vision, it's easy to lose motivation when budgeting gets challenging.

Beyond lacking goals, many people struggle with a fundamental misunderstanding about what budgeting actually provides: they see it as restriction rather than freedom.

4. Misunderstanding Freedom and Control

People associate discipline with limitations when really discipline frees you up.

There's a common misconception that budgeting restricts your freedom. Many people, especially in the Black community, resist budgeting because they don't want to feel controlled. "I'm grown, don't tell me how to spend my money" is a frequent response to the suggestion of budgeting.

What these people fail to understand is that true freedom comes through discipline, not through unrestrained spending. When you control your money through a budget, you gain the freedom to make intentional choices rather than being at the mercy of impulses and emergencies.

Another major obstacle to successful budgeting lies in how we connect money with our feelings. Money decisions should be logical, but many people make them emotionally.

5. Emotional Spending

Money decisions should be logical, but many people make them emotionally. They shop when they're bored, stressed, or anxious. Amazon becomes an easy escape from negative emotions, but it also quickly derails any budget.

To successfully budget, you must detach emotions from money management. This doesn't mean you can't enjoy spending on things you value, but it does mean your spending decisions should come from a place of thoughtful intention rather than emotional reaction.

Managing money effectively requires a certain emotional detachment. While money matters certainly affect our feelings, your budgeting decisions should come from a place of logic rather than emotional impulse. This separation between feelings and finances is essential for maintaining control over your money.

How Often to Review and Adjust Your Budget

Creating a budget is just the first step. Reviewing it consistently is what transforms it from a document into a powerful financial tool. Consistency forms the backbone of successful money management, allowing you to catch problems early and make timely adjustments as your financial situation evolves.

The question then becomes not whether to review your budget regularly, but exactly how frequently these check-ins should happen to maintain optimal control.

Review Frequency

At minimum, you should review your budget twice a month, which works well since most folks get paid biweekly or twice a month anyway. Each time money hits your account is a perfect chance to check in with your budget and make sure you're staying on track.

But honestly, you should review it as many times as you need to keep yourself in check. Some people, especially when you're just starting out or if your income varies from month to month, might need to look at that budget every couple of days. You got these things coming at you and maybe some extra money coming in here and there, so you gotta stay on top of it. Others who've been at this longer and have pretty stable money coming in might do fine with checking in just twice a month.

When to Make Adjustments

While reviewing your budget should happen frequently, making adjustments to the budget itself typically occurs less often—usually monthly or bimonthly. However, there are two specific situations that always warrant budget adjustments:

1. **When your income changes** (either increases or decreases)

2. **When your variable expenses significantly change**

When you first start budgeting, you'll likely need to make more frequent adjustments as you learn what your actual spending looks like in various categories. You might not know exactly how much your electric bill will be or how much you truly spend on gas each month. As you gather this data over time, your budget will become more accurate and require fewer adjustments.

Your budget has to be fluid. It has to be something that is flexible to an extent because money changes.

Remember that adjustments aren't a sign of failure. They're a sign that you're actively managing your money and responding to real-life circumstances. A budget that never changes is probably not an accurate reflection of your financial life.

Now that you understand how to maintain your budget, let's talk about creating a budgeting system that truly belongs to you, not just using whatever tools happen to be available.

Creating Your Own Budgeting System

I want people to develop their own budgeting system. And part of the reason I want you to develop your own system is because I want you to be in the habit of building, creating and producing.

I like having a system that's separated from the system. What do I mean by that? Your checking account, savings, and online banking tools—that's one system. But I want you to develop your own separate budgeting system. Don't just rely on what your bank app tells you you've spent.

When you build your own budgeting system—whether that's a spreadsheet, a notebook, or some other method— you take ownership of the process. This separation gives you true control rather than just passively tracking what's already happened.

I've personally done a written budget every single month since 1992 when I went off to college. I got my first apartment in August of 1992, and I had to do a budget right away. I even had to go down and get food stamps at first. That's where my budgeting journey began. Not from a place of financial comfort, but from genuine necessity.

My budgeting tools have evolved over time—from those little hardback ledger books you get from Office Max to Google spreadsheets since about 2017—but the consistent practice of creating and maintaining my own system has been instrumental in my financial journey.

Moving Forward with Intention

Budgeting is more than a financial exercise. It's a fundamental shift in how you relate to money. When you create and follow a budget, you're declaring that you are in charge of your financial life. You're taking your position as the manager, with money as your employee.

This position of control brings both power and peace. It eliminates the stress and anxiety that come from financial uncertainty and replaces them with confidence and clarity.

As we move forward, we'll build on this foundation of control by establishing your first concrete financial goal: creating an initial emergency fund. If you've been wondering what you're actually budgeting for, this next step will give you a clear, achievable target that will further strengthen your financial position.

But you can't reach that goal without first establishing control through a budget. The budget is your roadmap, showing you exactly where you are and plotting the course to where you want to go. Without it, you're just wandering financially, hoping to somehow arrive at wealth.

Take control of your money now. Don't let another day pass where your money controls you.

Chapter 3

Your First Line of Defense: Building a $3,000 Safety Net

How a Small Safety Net Prevents Financial Disaster

Imagine this: It's 11 PM on a Sunday night.

Your refrigerator makes a strange clicking sound, then goes silent. By morning, everything inside is warming up.

$300 worth of groceries you just bought, spoiling before your eyes.

And payday? That's five days away.

For most Americans, this isn't just a hypothetical scenario. It's a financial nightmare they're just one unexpected event away from facing. I've seen it happen countless times: a $500 car repair sending someone into a financial tailspin that takes months to recover from. When you've got no safety net, minor inconveniences become major catastrophes.

That's why, now that you have your budget in place from Chapter 2, it's time to establish your first concrete financial goal: building an initial emergency fund of $3,000.

This isn't just another financial task. It's your financial seatbelt. You don't put on a seatbelt because it's comfortable or convenient—you put it on just in case. As I always say, "It's better to be prepared and not have an emergency than to not be prepared and have an emergency."

Understanding the Purpose of Your Initial Emergency Fund

An initial emergency fund is your safety net—a financial buffer that ensures if something unexpected happens, you can cover it without derailing your entire financial plan.

Think of your financial journey like building a house. This $3,000 fund isn't the entire house, it's the temporary structure that protects your construction site while you work on the foundation. It's a "stop gap" that holds you over while you're doing other foundational financial work, ensuring that a sudden rainstorm (unexpected expense) doesn't wash away your progress.

This initial protection isn't your full emergency fund (we'll get to that in Chapter 6), but it helps you sleep better at night knowing you can handle small emergencies upfront. With this safety net in place, you won't need to resort to payday loans, borrowing from your 401k, credit card debt, or awkward conversations asking friends and family for money when unexpected expenses arise. Instead, you'll have peace of mind and the financial flexibility to handle life's inevitable surprises.

True Emergencies vs. "Want" Emergencies

Before we go further, let's clarify something important: an emergency fund is for actual emergencies—not wants disguised as emergencies. This distinction trips up many people who blur the lines between needs and wants, often intentionally.

Examples of true emergencies:

- Car repairs (flat tires, brake problems)

- Essential home appliance failures (refrigerator, heating system)

- Unexpected medical bills

- Critical emergency home repairs

- Job loss or reduced income (where I live, unemployment only pays about $250 a week—hardly enough to cover basic necessities. Your emergency fund bridges that gap until you find new employment)

Not emergencies:

- Concert tickets (*"But it's Beyoncé!"*)

- Vacation opportunities (*"I need this for my mental health!"*)

- Sales at your favorite stores (*"But it's 50% off!"*)

- The latest electronics or fashion items

The emergency fund is designed specifically to protect you from unexpected problems, not to fund unexpected opportunities for enjoyment. This distinction requires discipline and clarity about what constitutes a genuine need versus a want.

The Dangers of Not Having Emergency Savings

Not having emergency savings is like driving without a seatbelt on a winding mountain road during a thunderstorm. You might make it safely to your destination, but one unexpected curve could send you into a financial disaster with consequences that ripple through every aspect of your life.

The stress alone of knowing you have no buffer between you and financial catastrophe can affect your health, relationships, and daily peace of mind, but the practical consequences are even more severe when that inevitable emergency arrives. Let me show you how quickly small problems escalate when you have no financial safety net.

1. Minor Inconveniences Become Major Catastrophes

This is perhaps the most important point to understand. When you don't have emergency savings, small problems quickly escalate into financial disasters. A $500 car repair isn't much in the big picture of your financial life, but if you don't have that $500 available, it might as well be

$5,000 or even $50,000. You'll be forced to take drastic measures to cover it.

2. Constant Financial Stress and Anxiety

Living without a financial safety net means living with a constant low-level (or high-level) anxiety. Every unexpected expense becomes a potential crisis. This stress affects your mental health, your relationships, and even your physical wellbeing.

3. Resorting to Harmful Financial Products

Without emergency savings, many people turn to payday loans, high-interest credit cards, or predatory lending options that can charge 300-400% interest when annualized. These "solutions" often create bigger long-term problems than the original emergency.

4. Repeatedly Starting Over

One of the most frustrating dangers is constantly having to restart your wealth-building journey. Let's say you've built up $5,000 in investments, but then your car needs a $3,000 repair. Without an emergency fund, you might have to liquidate investments, possibly paying penalties and taxes, which sets your wealth-building progress back significantly.

5. Inability to Focus on Long-Term Financial Goals

When you're constantly putting out financial fires, you can't focus on building wealth. Your attention and resources are diverted to survival mode rather than growth mode.

Now that you understand the real dangers of not having an emergency fund, you're probably thinking, "Okay, I'm convinced—but where do I find the money?" Let's dive into practical steps that will help you build this crucial safety net, even if you think every dollar is already accounted for.

Practical Ways to Find $3,000 for Your Emergency Fund

Building that initial $3,000 might seem daunting, especially if you're living paycheck to paycheck right now. But I've helped hundreds of people find money they didn't know they had, hidden in plain sight within their current finances. The following six steps will guide you through uncovering and redirecting money toward your emergency fund, even if you think every dollar is already accounted for.

Step 1 - Know Your Numbers

The foundation of finding discretionary income is knowing exactly what comes in and what goes out. This is where your zero-based budget from Chapter 2 becomes crucial. When you put your finances on paper, you often discover money you didn't realize you had.

When you put your finances on paper through your zero-based budget, something remarkable happens—what I call "financial epiphanies." People often have a vague idea they bring home $3,000 and spend $2,500, but when they actually track it on paper, they discover they're only spending $2,200. Suddenly, they realize they have $800 of discretionary income, not $500!

I've seen this happen countless times. The moment when someone's eyes widen as they discover money they didn't know they had simply by putting their finances on paper. You can't save what you don't know you have, and your budget reveals the truth.

With your numbers clearly laid out, you can now take the next crucial step: honestly separating your true needs from your wants.

Step 2 - Distinguish Between Needs and Wants

Within your budget, clearly separate true needs from wants. This isn't about eliminating all wants. It's about making conscious decisions about them. Ask yourself: "Among these wants, how do I want to spend my discretionary income? Can I reduce my 'want' spending from $300 to $200 per month to free up an extra $100 for my emergency fund?"

Being honest about which expenses are truly necessary versus which are optional is often eye-opening and can free up significant amounts of money.

Once you've identified which expenses are truly needs versus wants, it's time to get even more specific by finding and eliminating the hidden money drains in your budget.

Step 3 - Plug the Money Leaks

Conduct a thorough audit of your spending to find and eliminate financial waste:

- **Cancel unused subscriptions:** Those $9.99 monthly charges add up quickly.

- **Reduce food waste:** The average American family throws away about 25% of the food they buy.

- **Cut back on eating out:** Even reducing by one meal per week can save $50-$100 monthly.

- **Examine your shopping habits:** You shouldn't be on a first-name basis with the Amazon delivery person!

- **Review insurance policies:** You might be over-insured or paying for coverage you no longer need.

- **Audit your cell phone plan:** Many people pay for data or services they never use.

After addressing the obvious spending leaks, let's look at another often-overlooked area where you might find hidden money: your employment benefits and withholdings.

Step 4 - Know Your Pay Stub

Review your employment benefits and withholdings carefully. Are you still paying for family health insurance when your children now have their own coverage? I kept the same health insurance plan for years without reviewing it, and I was paying for coverage I no longer needed!

Maybe you're withholding too much for taxes and giving the government an interest-free loan. Check your retirement contributions—are they optimized? These seemingly small adjustments can free up hundreds of dollars monthly that you never realized were available.

After addressing your existing income and expenses, let's explore another powerful strategy: creating additional income streams using skills you already possess.

Step 5 - Consider a Side Hustle

Almost everyone has marketable skills or talents they take for granted, often giving away for free what others would gladly pay for. Take an honest inventory of what you do well that others might struggle with or activities you enjoy that could translate into extra income, then consider how to monetize these abilities in your spare time.

Here are some common examples of skills people overlook that could become sources of extra cash:

- Are you making peach cobblers for everyone at church for free? Start charging $20 each.

- Do you have handyman skills? Offer your services for a reasonable fee.

- Can you tutor, write, design, or provide other skilled services? The gig economy makes it easier than ever to monetize your talents.

Even an extra $200-$300 per month can dramatically accelerate your progress in building up your emergency fund.

With both expense reduction and potential income increases identified, there's one final strategy that will practically guarantee your success: changing how you think about saving.

Step 6 - Make Saving a Bill

Instead of saving whatever's left after paying your bills (which often means saving nothing), make saving your FIRST "bill." This distinction is crucial. Don't put savings at the bottom of your budget priority list; put it at the TOP.

Once you know you have $500 in monthly discretionary income, automatically transfer that money to savings immediately when you get paid, not at the end of the month when it's likely already spent. If you need to make adjustments afterward, adjust your other expenses. This psychological shift changes everything: instead of treating savings as optional, you're making it non-negotiable. Don't save what's left after spending; spend what's left after saving.

Why $3,000 and How Quickly You Should You Save It

Now that you understand how to find the money for your emergency fund, you might be wondering why I specifically recommend $3,000 as your initial target. This amount isn't random or pulled out of thin air. It's chosen for practical reasons based on what I've seen work for hundreds of people. Let me explain why this specific figure matters and the realistic timeframe for achieving it.

The Magic of $3,000

There's nothing mystical about the $3,000 figure, but it's a carefully chosen target amount for several practical reasons:

1. **It covers most common emergencies:** Most appliance replacements, car repairs, and medical co-pays fall under $3,000.

2. **It's achievable:** Unlike a full emergency fund (which might be $10,000-$20,000), $3,000 feels attainable to most people.

3. **It significantly reduces financial stress:** Even this initial amount provides enough security to eliminate many financial worries.

4. **It prevents most debt emergencies:** With $3,000 saved, you can handle most unexpected expenses without resorting to debt.

5. **It builds momentum:** Having $3,000 already saved gives you a head start toward your full emergency fund *(which we'll cover in Chapter 6)*, creating psychological momentum.

There's something psychologically powerful about reaching that $3,000 milestone. I want you to feel the satisfaction of accomplishment along this journey. When you look at your account and see that $3,000 balance—money that's specifically designated for emergencies—it creates a sense of pride and security that's hard to describe until you've experienced it.

If your full emergency fund goal is $12,000, having that first $3,000 is incredibly motivating. It's like saying, "I'm already a quarter of the way there!" This emotional boost shouldn't be underestimated. It provides the momentum to keep going when the journey gets tough.

Setting a Realistic Timeline for Building Your Initial Emergency Fund

When clients ask me how fast they should build their emergency fund, I resist giving a one-size-fits-all answer because your financial journey is unique.

If you're working minimum wage with tight margins, a realistic timeline might be 6 months of consistent saving. On the other hand, if you have more income flexibility or can dramatically cut expenses, you might reach your goal in just 1-2 months with focused intensity.

The specific timeline isn't as important as having a concrete plan and sticking to it.

Whether it takes you 2 months or 6 months to reach your $3,000 goal, the important thing is that you're making consistent progress toward financial security. This initial safety net doesn't just protect you today, it creates the stability you need to take on the next critical challenge in your financial journey.

How $3,000 in Savings Enables Further Financial Progress

Building your initial $3,000 emergency fund is like laying the first level of bricks in your financial foundation. It won't protect you from every financial storm, but it will shield you from the most common financial disruptions that derail many people's progress.

With this safety net in place, you'll experience an immediate reduction in financial stress and gain the confidence that comes from knowing you can handle life's inevitable surprises. You'll sleep better at night knowing that a flat tire or broken appliance won't send your finances into a tailspin.

Most importantly, this initial emergency fund provides the stability you need to tackle the next critical step in building your financial foundation: eliminating the bad debt that's holding you back from true financial freedom. Without this safety net, you'd be constantly vulnerable to new debt even as you try to eliminate existing debt.

In the next chapter, we'll focus on identifying and eliminating the bad debt that's preventing you from building wealth. With your $3,000 emergency fund in place, you'll be able to make consistent progress on debt elimination without being derailed by life's unexpected expenses.

Chapter 4

Breaking the Chains: Eliminating the Debt That Keeps You Poor

Understanding the Restrictions Debt Places on Your Life

That knot in your stomach when the bills arrive. The constant mental math, figuring out which payment you can delay this month. The sleepless nights wondering how you'll ever get ahead when so much of your paycheck is already spoken for before you earn it.

Debt doesn't just drain your bank account. It steals your peace, your options, and your future.

What if I told you that the difference between struggling financially and building real wealth isn't how much you make, but whether you're trapped in the cycle of debt?

Imagine two homes side by side in your neighborhood—one being built from the ground up, the other being demolished. The same construction crew moves back and forth between sites. Every minute they spend tearing down the old house is time they can't invest in building the new one.

This is exactly what happens with your money when you're carrying bad debt. You can't build wealth while simultaneously being weighed down by obligations that drain your resources. The payments you make toward debt are payments you can't invest in your future.

With our budgeting system established and an initial $3,000 safety net in place, it's time to focus on what may be the most transformative step in your financial journey: eliminating the debt that's holding you back from everything you want to achieve.

The Types of Debt That Harm Your Financial Future

Bad debt is any debt on anything that is not increasing in value. It's debt attached to items that are either depreciating or not appreciating at all. Understanding this distinction matters because not all debt impacts your financial future the same way.

Common examples of bad debt include:

- **Student loans** - While education may increase your earning potential over time, the actual debt doesn't attach to any physical asset that grows in value, making it a financial burden that can follow you for decades without building equity.

- **Credit card balances** - These typically fund everyday purchases, dining out, entertainment, or clothing that provides temporary enjoyment but depreciates or is consumed immediately, leaving you paying interest on items long after their usefulness has ended.

- **Medical bills** - Though absolutely necessary for your health and wellbeing, these expenses don't create any financial asset in return, yet the debt can linger for years, draining resources that could be building wealth elsewhere.

- **Car loans** - That new vehicle loses 20-30% of its value the moment you drive it off the lot and continues depreciating while you're making payments, meaning you're financing an asset that's actively shrinking in value each month.

- **Personal loans** for vacations, weddings, or consumer purchases - These experiences and celebrations may create wonderful memories, but they generate no financial return while the debt remains long after the event has passed, creating a financial anchor that drags down your wealth-building potential.

When evaluating any debt, ask yourself: "Is this debt attached to something that's going up in value?" If not, you're looking at bad debt that needs to be eliminated.

Why Bad Debt Destroys Wealth Building

Bad debt is a wealth killer, plain and simple. It locks you into a cycle of payments that keeps you spinning your wheels instead of moving forward. I've seen people making six figures who are broke because they're drowning in payments on stuff that's not building them any wealth. You can't get ahead when you're throwing money at things going down in value. That's just not how wealth works.

How Splitting Financial Resources Slows All Progress

Think about it like this: when you're paying off debt, your money is working against you, not for you. Going back to our construction analogy, every dollar directed toward debt payments is a dollar that can't work for you in building wealth. Your financial resources are divided, with a significant portion dedicated to tearing down rather than building up.

If you spend 25 years paying off bad debt, that's 25 years you could have been building significant wealth instead. For example, if your construction crew spends 25 years tearing down that old house, they'll never get to build anything on the empty lot next door. In those same 25 years, you could have built multiple properties, developed entire neighborhoods, maybe even constructed 17 skyscrapers with all that time and resources.

How Financing Multiplies the Real Price of Everything You Buy

Another way debt kills your wealth-building potential is by making everything cost more than it should. When you finance purchases with bad debt, you never pay just the sticker price. That $30,000 car actually costs you $42,000 or more after interest.

Building wealth isn't just about earning money, it's about keeping what you earn. Interest and fees represent money that leaves your pocket forever, preventing you from building your net worth.

How Debt Removes Your Freedom to Choose

Beyond just the numbers, debt takes something even more valuable from you – your freedom. The ultimate goal of building wealth is freedom. The ability to make choices based on what you want rather than what you're obligated to do. Bad debt does the opposite. The borrower is a slave to the lender.

When carrying bad debt, you're locked into payment obligations that restrict your options. You may need to stay on a job you dislike because you have to make those payments. You might be unable to pursue opportunities that could dramatically improve your life because you're tied to your debt obligations. This isn't freedom. It's financial servitude.

You're locked into a contract that says you have to pay that $600 a month for that car. They got you hook, line and sinker—locked in like an indentured servant. You spend your time working for that car instead of working to build wealth for yourself.

The Psychological Price You Pay When Carrying Debt

And let's talk about what debt does to you mentally. The stress and anxiety that come with debt shouldn't be underestimated. Carrying bad debt negatively impacts your thought process, your stress levels, and your anxiety. It affects your feeling of safety, comfort, and confidence. It begins to wreak havoc on you as a person and your mental health.

This burden affects every aspect of your life, from sleep quality to personal relationships.

Why Debt Creates a Compounding Effect in the Wrong Direction

While debt is draining you mentally, it's also doing something mathematically dangerous to your money. Most people only think about compounding when it comes to investments, but here's the truth: compounding works in both wealth and debt.

Every month you owe debt, you're not only paying interest that compounds against you, but you're also missing out on what that money could be earning if it was invested instead.

When you're paying on debt, you're getting hit twice. You're losing money to interest and fees while also missing out on potential investment returns. This completely changes your financial future over time. And this compounding problem directly impacts how much you're actually worth.

How Debt Directly Reduces Your Net Worth

Calculating your net worth is simple:

Assets - Liabilities = Net Worth

Every bad debt you carry is a liability that directly reduces your net worth. The point of building wealth is to build assets that you own, not build liabilities that you owe. But how do you break free from this wealth-destroying cycle? The answer lies in a systematic approach to eliminating your debts once and for all.

How The Debt Snowball Method Can Lead You to Financial Freedom

So we've seen how bad debt locks you into payments, robs you of freedom, stresses you out, and keeps your money working against you instead of for you. The good news is there's a proven way to break free from this trap and get your money working for you again.

I've helped hundreds of people eliminate their debt through "The Debt Snowball Method", and it works not just mathematically but psychologically too.

How the Debt Snowball Method Works

The debt snowball is a specific process that I use with my clients to knock out debt systematically. Think of it as a tool that not only eliminates your financial obligations but also builds your confidence with each win along the way.

Let me break down exactly how you can put this method to work starting today.

1. **List all your debts from smallest to largest balance**—don't worry about interest rates

2. **Pay minimum payments on all debts** every month to stay current

3. **Attack the smallest debt first** with all your available discretionary income from your budget

4. **Once the smallest debt is paid off,** take the minimum payment you were making on that debt plus the extra money you were applying to it, and roll that combined amount to the next debt on your list

5. **Repeat this process,** rolling payments together as each debt is eliminated, until all debts are paid off

Before you begin your debt snowball journey, make sure you've completed your initial $3,000 emergency fund from Chapter 3. This is critical. You need that safety net in place first.

Only after you've secured your initial savings should you redirect your discretionary income toward attacking debt. This proper sequence ensures you won't be derailed by small emergencies while working on your debt elimination.

The key to making your debt snowball powerful is starting with as much discretionary income as possible. This is why being ultra-specific with your budget is so important. The more you can free up from your monthly expenses and the more extra income you can generate, the faster you'll eliminate each debt.

Look for ways to increase your discretionary income - trim expenses further, sell things you don't need, or add a temporary side hustle. The more money you have available to put toward debt elimination, the more momentum your snowball will have from the beginning.

The spreadsheet for your debt snowball plan can calculate how long it will take to become debt-free. The reason it's called a snowball is you gain momentum. By the time you get to that last debt, if you have three or four debts, you're paying $1,200, $1,500, or $2,000 a month toward that debt to pay it off quickly.

The Debt Snowball vs The Debt Avalanche

Some financial experts recommend the "avalanche method," which prioritizes debts by interest rate, tackling the highest-interest debts first. While this approach saves more money mathematically over the long term, it overlooks a crucial factor: human psychology.

Some people get hung up on interest rates, arguing that paying the highest-interest debt first saves more money. But here's what I've learned: if you drag out your debt payoff for 10 years, yes, interest becomes a big issue. But if you attack your debt with intensity and knock it out in two or three years, the interest difference between the two methods becomes minimal. The psychological benefits of the snowball method far outweigh the small amount of interest you might save with the avalanche approach when you're committed to quick debt elimination.

Personal finance isn't just about numbers, it's about behavior. The debt snowball method recognizes that people need to see progress quickly to stay motivated. By paying off smaller debts first, you experience early wins that boost your confidence and reinforce your commitment to becoming debt-free.

If you can knock out a $500 credit card debt and a $700 debt in two or three months, you'll feel an immediate sense of accomplishment. These early victories create momentum that carries you through the longer process of paying off larger debts.

A lot of people don't have vision. They can't see long term, but most people can see three or four weeks or a month or two down the road. Getting those early wins keeps the momentum going. They build confidence quickly and create better long-term focus. It helps with the behavior and the natural emotion of money if we can knock out some of the small debts first.

You gotta stack wins in this game. The way you build momentum is by getting those early wins under your belt. For example, you already started doing your budget and you already built that initial savings. Now you knock out a couple small debts quickly. All of a sudden you start to see yourself accomplishing things. Those credit cards that have been hanging over your head for five years are gone in two months. Now you're rolling for real.

The beautiful thing is your money is snowballing, but more importantly, YOU are snowballing too. Your confidence starts growing. Your motivation kicks in stronger. Your inspiration to finish this journey multiplies. Everything about you starts snowballing right alongside your debt plan.

The Long-Term Price I Paid for Postponing Debt Payoff

I was in student loan debt until I was 51 years old. When I was in my twenties, back in 2000, my wife and I had a combined student loan debt of $50,000—I had $25,000, and she had $25,000.

Instead of aggressively paying it off, we did deferments and got on slow payment plans. By 2012, that $50,000 had ballooned to over $70,000 because of interest and delayed payments. We didn't finally pay it off until 2021.

Looking back, I can see how much wealth-building opportunity we missed during those two decades. If we had eliminated that debt earlier and redirected those payments into investments, our financial situation would be dramatically different today.

Don't make the same mistake I did. Address your bad debt head-on and eliminate it as quickly as possible so you can move on to building real wealth. My story shows what happens when you delay. Now let me show you exactly how to avoid my path and take control of your debt situation today.

Practical Steps to Implement Your Debt Snowball

Your success with the debt snowball directly connects to how well you implemented the previous steps. The detailed budget from Chapter 2 identifies your discretionary income. The discipline you developed saving your initial $3,000 emergency fund in Chapter 3 built the financial muscles you'll now use to tackle debt. Each step builds on the previous one. The better you get at controlling your money through budgeting and the faster you build your initial savings, the more prepared you are to make rapid progress through your debt snowball.

1. **Create a complete list of all debts** - Gather every statement and document every debt you owe, no matter how small or large.

2. **Organize debts from smallest to largest balance** - Focus solely on the total amount owed, not interest rates.

3. **Ensure you're making minimum payments on everything** - Stay current on all obligations to avoid late fees and credit damage.

4. **Calculate your discretionary income** - Using your zero-based budget from Chapter 2, determine exactly how much extra money you can put toward debt each month.

5. **Create a visual debt snowball plan** - Whether on paper or spreadsheet, map out how long it will take to eliminate each debt when applying your discretionary income plus the rolled payments from previous debts.

6. **Track your progress visibly** - Create a visual reminder of your progress, perhaps by coloring in a debt thermometer as you eliminate each obligation.

7. **Celebrate small victories** - Acknowledge each debt you eliminate; these celebrations reinforce the positive behavior.

8. **Stay focused until complete** - Maintain intensity until you've eliminated all bad debt, even when the process takes longer with larger debts.

Your debt snowball plan must be written out clearly. I'm a big believer in putting things on paper—whether that's a physical notebook or a digital spreadsheet doesn't matter, but you need to see it written out. There's something powerful about following a debt elimination plan that you can see and track. Don't try to keep this in your head. Write out the complete plan showing each debt, payment amounts, and projected payoff dates. Then follow that written plan religiously.

When you follow these practical steps consistently, something powerful begins to happen beyond just the numbers changing on your statements. You start experiencing a psychological transformation that accelerates your entire financial journey.

How Eliminating Debt Creates Both Financial and Personal Freedom

As you progress through your debt snowball, something remarkable happens: you begin to stack wins. Each debt you eliminate becomes not just a financial victory but a psychological one. Your financial confidence grows alongside your improving financial position.

By the time you've eliminated several debts, your attitude toward money changes. What once seemed impossible—

becoming completely debt-free—starts to feel inevitable. This confidence spills over into other areas of your financial life, making you more disciplined with spending, more intentional with saving, and more strategic with your resources. But the ultimate reward goes beyond even these psychological benefits. It's the complete financial freedom waiting for you on the other side of debt.

Imagine waking up tomorrow with no bad debt. No credit card payments, no student loans, no car payments—just the freedom to direct your resources toward building wealth and creating the life you want.

This isn't a fantasy. By systematically eliminating your bad debt through the snowball method, you will reach this milestone. The process might take months or even a few years, but the freedom waiting on the other side is worth every sacrifice along the way.

With bad debt eliminated, you'll be ready to move to the next phase of building your financial foundation: establishing strong credit. While we've focused on eliminating bad debt, having good credit will be essential for certain wealth-building strategies involving appreciating assets.

But first, you need to free yourself from the weight of bad debt that's currently preventing your financial growth. Start your debt snowball today, and take the next crucial step toward financial freedom.

You can't build and deconstruct at the same time. Choose to build your financial future by eliminating the debt that's holding you back.

You're halfway through—if you want to accelerate your money transformation, the full course walks you through exactly how. Check out my Smart Money Bro course right now at SmartMoneyBroU.com.

Chapter 5

Credit Mastery: Creating Financial Strength Without Financial Risk

Why Credit Should Be a Strategic Tool Not a Way of Life

When it comes to financial success, there's a tool many people misuse, misunderstand, or fear altogether—credit. Let me be clear from the start: credit itself won't make you wealthy. However, poor credit can certainly keep you poor. This distinction is crucial as we build the fifth piece of your financial foundation.

In the previous chapter, we focused on eliminating bad debt—getting rid of financial obligations that were holding you back. Now that you've cleared those obstacles, it's time to establish strong credit as a strategic tool for your wealth-building journey.

Credit, when used properly, serves one primary purpose in your wealth-building strategy: helping you purchase appreciating assets at better terms. It's not for everyday spending, impulse purchases, or funding a lifestyle you can't afford. It's simply a tool in your financial toolbox—and like any tool, its value depends entirely on how you use it.

How Consistent Payment Behavior Reflects Financial Character

The most effective strategy for building strong credit might seem obvious, but it's where most people fall short: pay your bills in full and on time, every time.

This goes beyond numbers on a credit report. It's about integrity and character. When we build good money habits, we simultaneously build good life habits. Being a person of your word matters tremendously in financial management.

You must become trustworthy to yourself with your money. For example, if a good friend handed you $10,000 to manage for a couple of years, you would treat that responsibility with great care. You would watch that money carefully, check on it regularly, and make sound decisions.

Yet many people don't bring that same level of integrity to managing their own money. The foundation of strong credit begins with this personal integrity. Especially, consistently meeting your financial obligations on time.

This personal integrity with payments forms the bedrock of your credit reputation. But integrity alone isn't enough. You also need awareness of where you currently stand in the credit landscape.

Why Understanding Your Current Credit Status Is Essential

You can't improve what you don't measure. Another critical strategy for building strong credit is understanding your current credit situation.

Pull your full credit reports regularly. Federal law entitles you to free credit reports annually from each major bureau through AnnualCreditReport.com. Services like Credit Karma also provide regular updates and monitoring.

When reviewing your credit reports, look carefully for:

- Late payments
- Errors or inaccuracies
- Accounts in collections
- Accounts you don't recognize
- Old debts that should have fallen off your report

Credit reporting agencies must correct errors, but they won't know about them unless you identify and dispute them. Don't be passive about your credit report. Feel free to dispute old collections and items that shouldn't be there.

Many people don't realize they have the right to challenge incorrect information. If you spot something questionable—especially old collections that should have aged off your report—dispute it immediately. The credit bureaus are required to investigate and remove inaccurate information, but they won't do this automatically. You must be proactive in cleaning up your credit report.

How Credit Protection Creates Surprising Financial Benefits

In 2012, my social security number was stolen and used to file a fraudulent tax return. I didn't discover this until I tried to file my own taxes that year. After resolving that situation, I took the precautionary step of freezing my credit.

I didn't just freeze it temporarily. I kept it frozen for nearly 13 years until 2025. During that entire period, I only unfroze it once for about two days in 2014 when I needed to refinance my primary residence. Then I immediately froze it again. This might seem extreme to some, but it gave me peace of mind knowing that no one could open new accounts in my name.

During those years, I didn't check my credit regularly because I knew I wasn't planning to make any major purchases that would require credit. However, I continued paying all my bills on time. When I finally checked my credit score after unfreezing it, it was nearly 800, simply because of consistent on-time payments over the years.

This demonstrates an important principle: consistent good behavior over time builds excellent credit, even when you're not actively trying to 'game' the credit scoring system. My experience shows how consistent payment behavior impacts your credit score over time. While payment history is the most important factor, it's not the only one. Another key element that affects your credit score is utilization.

Understanding How Credit Utilization Impacts Your Credit Score

Credit utilization—the percentage of your available credit that you're currently using—plays a significant role in your credit score. For example, if you have a $1,000 credit limit and your balance is $300, your utilization ratio is 30%.

Lower utilization ratios generally lead to better credit scores. Financial experts typically recommend keeping utilization below 30%, but for optimal credit scores, aim for single-digit utilization.

However, I want to emphasize something even more important than the numbers. The temptation factor with credit cannot be overstated. You must approach credit with extreme precaution and extreme discretion.

I'm not being dramatic when I emphasize the word 'extreme.' I've seen too many financially disciplined people fall into credit card traps, because credit gives you the dangerous ability to make purchases beyond your current means. Thus, creating an illusion of wealth that can quickly become a debt nightmare.

If you've struggled with financial discipline in the past, stay away from credit cards until you're confident in your ability to use them responsibly. This isn't about judgment, it's about protecting your financial foundation from potential damage. You need to be absolutely sure you can resist impulse purchases and pay balances in full every month before using credit cards.

The Step-by-Step Approach to Strategically Building Credit

For those who need to build credit from scratch or rebuild after past challenges, you need a systematic plan of attack. I'm going to give you a methodical approach that has worked for many people I've advised over the years. Follow these steps in order and you'll be on your way to establishing the credit foundation you need for wealth building.

1. **Practice financial responsibility with non-credit bills first.** Pay your utilities, rent, phone bill, and other monthly obligations on time to develop the habit of meeting payment deadlines.

2. **Start small with secured credit options** if necessary. A secured credit card (backed by a deposit) can be a good first step if you can't qualify for traditional credit.

3. **Use credit sparingly for necessary expenses** you would purchase anyway. Choose one regular,

budgeted expense like gas or groceries and use credit only for that specific purpose.

4. **Keep credit limits low initially** to reduce the temptation to overspend. You don't need a $10,000 limit when you're starting out—a $500 or $1,000 limit is sufficient for building credit while minimizing risk.

5. **Pay the balance in full each month** to avoid interest charges and demonstrate responsible usage.

6. **Monitor your credit reports regularly** for errors and dispute any inaccuracies promptly.

7. **Avoid applying for multiple forms of credit in a short timeframe**, as this can lower your score temporarily.

Building Wealth Without the Risk of Credit Card Dependency

I want to be transparent about my personal approach to credit card use. I don't use credit cards. I haven't had a credit card in about 12-13 years, and I don't miss them. I firmly believe in using credit only for purchasing appreciating assets—things that go up in value over time.

That said, I recognize many people use credit cards for everyday expenses, points, rewards, or convenience. My daughter is a good example. She wanted to build credit to eventually purchase property, an appreciating asset. Rather than telling her to avoid credit entirely, I helped her develop a disciplined approach.

We selected a credit card with a small limit, and I advised her to use it exclusively for one necessary expense: gas for her car. This way, she's building credit history with a predictable, budgeted expense she would have anyway, while avoiding the temptation to use credit for unnecessary purchases. By limiting the card to a single specific purpose, she's learning to view credit as a strategic tool rather than a source of additional spending money.

If you choose to use credit cards, you must be extremely disciplined. Pay your balance in full every month, don't spend money you don't have, and never use credit cards to finance a lifestyle beyond your means. The moment you start carrying balances from month to month, you've crossed from using credit as a tool to becoming a servant to debt. And never forget that the borrower is a slave to the lender.

My personal approach to credit cards stems from a broader philosophy about what credit truly represents in your financial life. Despite what popular culture might suggest, credit is not a status symbol.

The Power of Using Credit As a Wealth Tool Instead of a Status Symbol

Years ago, having credit cards was sometimes seen as a status symbol—a "flex" that demonstrated financial success. This perspective is both outdated and dangerous.

Credit is not a status symbol. It's simply a tool in your financial toolbox that helps you secure better terms when purchasing appreciating assets. Your credit score doesn't define your wealth or worth. It merely indicates how well you've managed borrowed money.

I want you to internalize this fundamental truth about credit in your wealth-building journey. Credit itself is not going to make you rich, but having bad credit can certainly keep you poor. This isn't just a catchy phrase, it's the framework for understanding credit's proper role in your financial life. Poor credit creates barriers to opportunities and forces you to pay more for everything from mortgages to insurance.

The purpose of building strong credit is not to access more consumer goods or to impress others. It's to position yourself for strategic wealth-building through property acquisition, business opportunities, and other appreciating assets.

Common Credit Mistakes to Avoid

As you work on establishing strong credit, you need to know what landmines to avoid. I've seen people make the same mistakes over and over again when trying to build their credit scores. Let me walk you through the most common credit pitfalls that can derail your progress if you're not careful.

1. **Late payments:** Even a single late payment can significantly impact your credit score and stay on your report for years.

2. **High utilization:** Maxing out credit cards or consistently carrying high balances relative to your limits hurts your score.

3. **Closing old accounts:** The length of your credit history matters, so keeping older accounts open (even if unused) can benefit your score.

4. **Applying for too much credit at once:** Multiple credit inquiries in a short period can temporarily lower your score.

5. **Co-signing without caution:** When you co-sign a loan, you're fully responsible for that debt if the primary borrower defaults. My philosophy is to NEVER co-sign.

6. **Ignoring your credit reports:** Not reviewing your reports regularly means errors might go unnoticed and uncorrected.

7. **Using credit for everyday consumption**: Be careful with this one. This habit can lead to accumulating debt and financial stress.

While avoiding these mistakes helps prevent damage to your credit, understanding the positive connection between credit and wealth creation is equally important. When used strategically, good credit becomes a powerful ally in building wealth.

Why Credit Strength Matters for Long-Term Wealth Creation

Having strong credit opens doors that remain closed to those with poor credit scores. When you maintain excellent credit, you gain specific financial advantages that directly impact your ability to build wealth. Let me show you exactly how strong credit helps accelerate your financial journey.

- Secure lower interest rates on mortgages for investment properties
- Qualify for business loans to fund business-building entrepreneurial ventures
- Obtain better terms when financing other appreciating assets
- Save thousands of dollars in interest over the life of necessary loans

- Avoid excessive security deposits for utilities and services

These advantages directly impact your ability to build wealth efficiently. For example, just a 1% difference in a mortgage interest rate can save you tens of thousands of dollars over the life of the loan. Money that can be redirected toward additional investments.

However, credit alone won't make you wealthy. It's merely an enabler that, when combined with sound financial management, disciplined saving, and strategic investing, helps accelerate your wealth-building journey.

Understanding this credit-wealth connection leads to an important question: exactly when should you use credit, and when should you avoid it? Having clear guidelines will help you make strategic decisions rather than emotional ones.

When to Use Credit and When to Avoid It

When it comes to using credit wisely, you need clear boundaries about what deserves financing and what should be paid with cash. Credit should usually be reserved exclusively for things that either appreciate in value or significantly increase your earning potential.

Here are the specific situations when using credit makes strategic sense:

- Purchasing a primary residence

- Acquiring investment properties

- Starting or expanding a business with positive cash flow projections

- Other investments with strong appreciation potential

Just as important as knowing when to use credit is understanding when to keep the credit cards in your wallet. Most people get into financial trouble because they use credit for things that provide temporary satisfaction but long term financial pain.

Here are the situations when you should absolutely avoid using credit, no matter how tempting it might seem:

- Everyday expenses you could pay with cash

- Depreciating assets like electronics and clothing

- Vacations and entertainment

- Covering regular bills when you're short on cash

- Impulse purchases

This distinction is crucial. Credit used for appreciating assets can help build wealth, while credit used for consumption typically destroys wealth over time.

The Strategic Role Credit Plays in Your Wealth Building System

Credit is merely a tool—neither inherently good nor bad. Its value depends entirely on how you use it.

Your goal isn't to have the highest possible credit score for its own sake, but rather to establish sufficient creditworthiness to access the resources needed for strategic wealth-building investments. Remember that excellent credit is not an achievement to celebrate in itself, but rather a stepping stone that helps you reach your true financial goals more efficiently. Remember, don't just "fix your credit" without addressing the behaviors that led to your poor credit in the first place.

With strong credit established, you're now ready for the final piece of your financial foundation: building a full emergency fund that provides complete security and peace of mind. This will be our focus in the next chapter, as we put the finishing touch on the solid financial base that will support your wealth-building journey for decades to come.

Chapter 6

Full Financial Security: Building Your Complete Emergency Fund

Why Financial Security Requires a Comprehensive Emergency Fund

When you've established good credit and completed the earlier steps in your financial foundation, you're ready to tackle one of the most powerful elements of financial security: the full emergency fund. This isn't just about having some money set aside. It's about creating true financial resilience that can withstand life's unexpected challenges.

Your initial $3,000 emergency fund was an excellent start, providing protection against minor emergencies and building your financial confidence. Now it's time to expand that protection to create comprehensive financial security.

Why Your Emergency Fund Should Cover Needs Not Wants

When financial advisors talk about emergency funds, you'll typically hear a common recommendation: have three to six months of expenses saved. But that advice needs more clarity. What expenses are we talking about exactly?

The industry standard is three to six months of your living expenses, but I like to be more specific: three to six months of your *needs*. And there's a reason for that. This is an emergency fund we're talking about, not a lifestyle maintenance fund.

This distinction is crucial. As much as you like to have your hair together with a fresh haircut and line up, or if you're a lady, you love the feeling of coming from the salon with your hair "done", —that's not really a need.

As much as you love spending that $100 a month going to the gym, it's not really a need, because you could do some pushups, some sit-ups, some squats, and walk and run without spending a penny - real talk.

That streaming service with all your favorite shows? Not a need. The premium cable package with all the sports channels? Not a need. Those are wants.

In a true emergency situation, you're focused on survival, not entertainment or convenience. Your emergency fund calculation should reflect that reality.

Your emergency fund isn't designed to maintain your lifestyle during challenging times, it's designed to keep you afloat and prevent financial disaster. When calculating what goes into your emergency fund, focus on true necessities:

- Housing (rent/mortgage)

- Utilities

- Food (groceries, not restaurants)

- Transportation (basic costs to get to work)

- Insurance premiums

- Essential medical expenses

Understanding what qualifies as a need versus a want is the first step. Now let's turn these needs into an actual dollar figure you can work toward—one that will provide real security when life gets complicated.

Calculating the Exact Amount Your Emergency Fund

To determine your full emergency fund target, return to your budget, that essential financial management tool we established earlier. Review your expenses and separate your needs from your wants.

The calculation is straightforward:

1. Identify your essential monthly expenses (needs only)

2. Multiply that figure by the number of months you want to cover (3-6 months)

3. Set this specific dollar amount as your emergency fund goal

If your expenses are about $3,000 a month, your emergency fund might be $9,000 for three months, $12,000 for four months, or $18,000 for six months. The math is simple, but the impact on your financial security is profound.

With your monthly needs figure in hand, the next question becomes: how many months should you actually cover? This isn't a one-size-fits-all answer. It depends on your specific circumstances and comfort with risk.

How Many Months Should You Save?

Between three and six months isn't just a random range. The right amount for you depends on your job stability, family situation, and how you personally feel about risk. Some people need more cushion to sleep well at night while others are comfortable with less.

3-4 months might be enough if:

- You work in a stable industry
- You have few or no dependents
- You have a job that you feel is fairly comfortable
- You have multiple income streams in your household

5-6 months (or more) makes sense if:

- Your income fluctuates (like if you're a writer or work on commission)

- You're the sole provider for your household

- You're self-employed or run your own business

- You work in an industry with frequent layoffs

If you're a person that has a strong intolerance for risk or you like to be extra careful, then you can feel free to have seven months of living expenses. I'm not mad at you. If you are an extreme person who is ultra careful and you just want the peace of mind of having eight months, I'm not gonna get too mad at you. Again, personal finance is personal, everybody's different.

Your risk tolerance is unique to you, and your emergency fund should reflect that. Some people can sleep just fine with three months saved, while others need more cushion to feel secure.

But I don't think you need more than that. You don't wanna have 9, 10, 12 months because you want that money working for you by building wealth instead of just sitting in a safe place.

Once you've determined your target amount—whether it's three months or eight—the next challenge is actually building that fund. Having a target is one thing; consistently moving toward it is another. Here's how to turn that goal into reality.

How to Systematically Build Your Full Emergency Fund

Transitioning from your initial $3,000 fund to a complete emergency fund requires strategy and commitment. How do you go from that initial emergency fund to a full one? Let me walk you through the practical steps that will get you there.

Building a full emergency fund takes focus. It takes discipline. It's not something that happens by accident or overnight. You have to be intentional about it every single day, every single paycheck.

The people who successfully build their emergency funds are the ones who make it a non-negotiable priority, not something they'll get to when it's convenient. This level of discipline is what separates those who achieve financial security from those who remain vulnerable.

Make It Automatic

The first step to building your emergency fund consistently is to take yourself out of the equation. Make sure you automate the payments. Treat it like a bill and it takes some of the guesswork out of it. When you automate it, you don't have to think about it. It just goes automatically into your account to build it up.

This approach removes the temptation to spend this money elsewhere. When you get paid, your emergency fund contribution should be automatically transferred before you have a chance to spend it.

Set Specific, Time-Bound Goals

Once you've set up your automation, you need to know exactly what you're working toward. Anytime you set a goal in this whole process, make sure you have action steps to go with the goal. When you set a goal, like for a full emergency fund, it should be specific and have time and amounts associated with it.

Saying "I want a full emergency fund" is not a goal. But if you wrote down "I want to save $18,000 by July of 2026," that's a goal that has a money amount and time element.

This specificity creates clarity and accountability. Without a clear target and deadline, your emergency fund becomes an abstract concept rather than an actionable plan.

Create an Action Plan

It's not enough just to have a goal. You have to have things in place that you're going to do. Such as habits that you're going to build to reach your goal. What are the 3-5 things you need to do on a daily, weekly, or monthly basis to reach your goal?

Your action steps might include:

- Setting up automatic transfers on paydays
- Committing to redirect tax refunds to your fund
- Dedicating a percentage of any extra income

- Regularly reviewing your budget for additional savings opportunities

These steps transform your goal from an aspiration to a practical plan with concrete actions.

Make Your Goal Visible

Creating an action plan is great, but you need to keep it front and center in your life. What I've found works best is making your goal unavoidable in your daily routine.

Put your goal somewhere you'll see it every single day. Maybe it's your phone screensaver, your computer desktop background, or a note stuck to your refrigerator door. You could get creative with this. For example, you might make a poster board with your emergency fund goal and milestone markers along the way. You could hang it right on your bathroom mirror so you'd see it morning and night while brushing your teeth.

The point isn't just to write down your goal once and forget about it. You need constant reminders of what you're working toward. When you see "$18,000 by December 2026" every day, it stays in your mind. You start making different choices. You think twice before dropping $50 on something you don't need because you remember that bigger goal.

Check in on your progress regularly too. I recommend setting a monthly reminder to review where you stand. Are you hitting the targets you set? Do you need to adjust your action steps? This regular review keeps you accountable and gives you chances to celebrate your wins along the way. Sometimes you'll be ahead of schedule, sometimes behind, but that consistent check-in is what keeps you moving forward.

Apply Extra Money

While your automatic transfers build your fund consistently, look for opportunities to accelerate your progress. Any unexpected money that comes your way is perfect for this purpose.

Got a tax refund? Don't blow it on something that won't matter in three months. Send a good chunk of it straight to your emergency fund. Same goes for work bonuses, birthday money, overtime pay, or that side hustle income. The faster you build your emergency fund, the sooner you'll have that safety net in place.

I'm not saying you can never enjoy extra money that comes your way. But before you spend it all, make a habit of asking yourself: "How much of this could help me reach my emergency fund goal faster?" Even directing half of any windfall toward your fund can dramatically cut down the time it takes to build your full safety net.

Where to Keep Your Emergency Fund

Once you're actively building your fund, you need to decide where to keep it. People overthink this part. I don't really care where you put the money so much, as long as it meets a few basic requirements.

Could it be in a high-yield savings account? Yes, that's okay. I like that. But understand something important: this is not your wealth-building money. This is not the money that's going to make you rich. This is part of your foundation, like the concrete slab under a house. It's not glamorous, but nothing stands without it.

Your emergency fund is a cornerstone of your financial house. Just like you wouldn't build a home on a weak foundation, you can't build lasting wealth without this protective layer in place. The emergency fund isn't about getting rich. It's about making sure you don't get knocked back to zero every time life throws something unexpected your way.

The money needs to be someplace where you can get to it quickly. Maybe a bank account, checking account, high-yield savings account, or money market account. The key is accessibility. If your car breaks down today and you need $800 to fix it, you can't wait three or four days for a transfer to process. You need that money immediately.

Don't worry so much about maximizing the interest rate. Yes, it's nice if your money earns something while it sits there, but that's not the primary purpose. We're going to build wealth with other money. This money is your safety net, not your growth engine.

The Psychological Impact of a Full Emergency Fund

The technical aspects of building an emergency fund are important, but let me tell you about something that doesn't get discussed enough: how it feels when you finally have one.

When I first saved up my full emergency fund of $30,000—about five or six months of my monthly expenses—man, that felt so good. I mean, I'm not sure if you understand how good that feels when you have a big stash of money that you can go to and you can pull from if needed.

There's a profound peace that comes with knowing you're prepared. You walk differently. You sleep better. You make decisions from a place of confidence rather than fear. When you have that cushion between you and life's emergencies, you stop living in constant anxiety about what might go wrong.

Think about it. Most people live paycheck to paycheck, where a $500 unexpected expense could derail their entire month. Every unusual sound their car makes brings dread. Every cough makes them worry about medical bills. That's no way to live.

With a full emergency fund, you're not bulletproof, but you're protected. You've created space between you and financial disaster. That psychological benefit is worth as much as the actual money in the account.

Maintaining Your Emergency Fund

Building your emergency fund is a major achievement, but your relationship with it doesn't end there. Once it's fully funded, you enter the maintenance phase.

First, protect it for true emergencies only. Be honest with yourself about what constitutes an emergency versus a want or an inconvenience. A broken refrigerator that needs replacement? Emergency. The latest phone model when yours still works fine? Not an emergency.

Second, if you do need to use your fund, make replenishing it your top financial priority. The protection it provides only works when it's fully funded. Treat it like a vital repair to your financial house that can't wait.

Third, adjust your fund as your life changes. If your essential expenses increase because you moved to a more expensive area or added family members, your emergency fund target should grow accordingly. The same three to six months of expenses might require more dollars than when you started.

Finally, review your emergency fund at least annually. Make sure it still aligns with your current situation and risk tolerance. As your overall financial picture improves, you might decide to adjust your target up or down based on your personal comfort level.

Common Mistakes to Avoid

I've seen people make the same mistakes with emergency funds over and over. Let me help you avoid them.

- **Confusing wants with needs when calculating the target amount.** Be ruthlessly honest about what constitutes a true need. In an actual emergency, you need housing, basic utilities, food, essential transportation, and critical medical care. You don't need entertainment subscriptions, dining out, or new clothes.

- **Borrowing from the emergency fund for non-emergencies.** Once you start dipping into this money for conveniences or opportunities, it's no longer serving its purpose. It becomes just another spending account. Keep that boundary firm.

- **Keeping too much in emergency savings.** Remember, money above your 6-8 month target could potentially work harder for you elsewhere. Once your emergency fund is complete, redirect your saving power toward wealth-building investments.

- **Setting it and forgetting it, not accounting for inflation or life changes.** Your $15,000 emergency fund from five years ago might not cover the same number of months today if your expenses have increased. Review and adjust periodically.

- **Using credit as a substitute for an actual emergency fund.** Credit cards, personal loans, or home equity are not emergency funds, they're debt that can compound your problems. True financial security comes from having your own money available, not borrowing capacity.

Avoiding these pitfalls ensures your emergency fund will actually be there when you need it most. A properly maintained emergency fund is the final piece of your solid financial foundation. It's the capstone that completes the groundwork for everything that follows.

How Your Emergency Fund Finalizes Your Financial Foundation

With a fully funded emergency fund, you've completed the essential foundation of your financial house. Think about what you've accomplished:

1. You've developed strong financial management habits

2. You've created and maintained a budget that gives you control

3. You've built an initial savings fund for smaller emergencies

4. You've eliminated bad debt that was holding you back

5. You've established strong credit as a wealth-building tool

6. You've created a comprehensive emergency fund

Most people never complete even half of these steps. The discipline and focus you've shown sets you apart from the crowd. You now have something that few Americans have: true financial security and a solid platform for building wealth.

These first six foundational steps provide the stability you need to begin growing significant wealth. The systems and safety nets you've established will support your financial growth for decades to come. You're not just managing money differently; you're positioned for an entirely different financial future.

But here's the truth: creating this foundation is just the beginning. The real challenge is making these practices a permanent part of your lifestyle. The financial foundation you've built isn't a temporary project; it's the base upon which you'll build lasting wealth and financial freedom. And that's exactly what we'll talk about next.

Chapter 7

The Lifestyle Shift: From Project to Permanent Practice

How to Make Good Financial Habits a Permanent Way of Life

You've made it. After six chapters of laying each brick of your financial foundation with care and precision, you now stand at a pivotal moment in your journey. The budget is created. The initial emergency fund is established. The bad debt is gone or on its way out. Your credit is strengthening. Your full emergency fund provides security.

So what comes next?

Many financial books end here, with the technical steps completed. But this isn't the end of your journey. It's actually the beginning of a new way of living.

The real challenge isn't in creating a budget or saving an emergency fund once. It's in making these practices a permanent part of your life—carving these money management habits in stone so they become as automatic as brushing your teeth or locking your door at night.

Wealth isn't a six-month event. It's a byproduct and result of your behavior over time. We're going to explore what it truly means to transform these financial principles from a temporary project into a lifelong lifestyle.

This transformation begins with understanding what it means to make discipline not just an occasional practice, but the foundation of how you approach money every day.

Why Financial Discipline Must Be Your Default Setting

Throughout this book, we've focused on the importance of discipline in managing your finances. Now it's time to understand that financial discipline isn't something you practice occasionally. It's a way of life.

Being Proactive vs. Reactive with Money

One of the clearest indicators that financial management has become your lifestyle is the shift from reactive to proactive behavior with money. When you're reactive, you're constantly responding to financial emergencies, past-due notices, and account overdrafts. You're always one step behind your money, chasing it rather than directing it.

Being proactive means you're in position to make financial decisions before they become urgent. You're planning next month's budget before this month ends. You're anticipating expenses rather than being surprised by them. You're setting money aside for future needs before they arise.

This proactive approach doesn't happen by accident. It's the result of deliberately practicing the principles we've discussed until they become second nature. It's about creating systems and processes that make good financial decisions your default mode rather than something you have to consciously force yourself to do.

Financial Security and Maturity

Financial maturity isn't about your age or income level. It's about your relationship with money. When financial management becomes your lifestyle, you demonstrate maturity in how you handle resources.

This maturity shows up when:

- You can delay gratification, understanding that some purchases are worth waiting for
- You make decisions based on long-term benefits rather than short-term satisfaction
- You value financial security over social approval
- You take responsibility for your financial choices rather than blaming circumstances
- You understand that wealth building is a marathon, not a sprint

These attributes don't develop overnight. They evolve as you consistently apply the principles of financial management over time. Eventually, these mature financial behaviors feel natural rather than forced, a clear sign that financial discipline has become your lifestyle.

Living Below Your Means

Perhaps the most powerful expression of financial discipline as a lifestyle is consistently living below your means—spending less than you earn regardless of how much you make.

This principle seems simple, but it's profoundly countercultural. We live in a society that encourages us to stretch to the limits of our income (and beyond) with car payments, housing costs, monthly subscriptions, and other expenses that consume every dollar as soon as it arrives.

When financial management becomes your lifestyle, you break free from this pattern mentally and behaviorally. You create a margin between your income and expenses. Not just during a temporary financial challenge or saving sprint, but as your normal way of living.

Living below your means doesn't mean living in deprivation. It means making intentional choices about where your money goes, prioritizing your true needs and most important wants while letting go of expenses that don't add real value to your life.

Controlling the Controllables

Life will always include uncertainties—economic downturns, unexpected expenses, health challenges, and other circumstances beyond your control. Financial discipline as a lifestyle means focusing your energy on what you can control rather than worrying about what you can't.

You can't control inflation, but you can control your spending.

You can't control the stock market, but you can control your saving rate.

You can't control the economy, but you can control your debt level.

You can't control your past financial mistakes, but you can control your current decisions.

This focus on controllable factors becomes a lifelong approach that provides peace even during turbulent times. Instead of feeling helpless when facing financial challenges, you turn your attention to the aspects of your finances where your decisions still make a difference.

Once you've embraced this disciplined mindset, the next step is ensuring these practices become permanent fixtures in your financial life and not just temporary solutions to immediate problems.

Making Financial Management Permanent

Most people get excited about building something new, but they struggle with the maintenance phase. They'll enthusiastically create a budget or start paying off debt, but when the initial excitement fades, so does their commitment. This is why so many financial journeys end prematurely.

From Temporary Project to Lifelong Practice

Financial management isn't something you do just to get out of debt, save for a house, or prepare for retirement. It's not a temporary diet you go on before returning to your normal eating habits. It's a fundamental shift in how you interact with money for the rest of your life.

Think of the steps we've covered as tools in your financial toolbox:

1. **Management mindset:** Understanding the importance of intentional financial management

2. **Budgeting system:** Creating and maintaining control over your money flow

3. **Initial emergency fund:** Establishing your first line of financial defense

4. **Debt elimination:** Removing the obstacles to wealth building

5. **Credit building**: Creating a strategic tool for acquiring appreciating assets

6. **Full emergency fund**: Completing your financial safety net

These tools aren't meant to be used once and then put away. They're meant to be permanent tools that you continue using throughout your financial journey. The budget isn't just for when money is tight. It's your ongoing plan for directing your resources. The emergency fund isn't just for when you're worried about job security. It's your permanent protection against life's uncertainties.

Sticking with the program means continuing these practices even when they no longer feel urgent. In fact, even more so when they no longer feel urgent. It's during the good times that many people abandon the very habits that created their financial stability, setting themselves up for problems when challenges return.

Processes, Systems, and Habits Produce Automatic Results

One of the most powerful aspects of making financial management a lifestyle is that over time, good results begin to happen automatically. When your systems are firmly established, wealth building becomes the natural outcome rather than something you have to constantly force.

Think about other areas of your life where habits produce results. If you brush and floss your teeth twice daily for years, good dental health happens almost automatically. If you exercise regularly for years, physical fitness becomes your normal state. In the same way, when you consistently follow sound financial practices, financial stability and growing wealth become your default position.

This automaticity develops because:

- Regular behaviors become habits that require minimal conscious effort

- Systems create guardrails that prevent major financial mistakes

- Processes ensure important financial tasks don't fall through the cracks

- Consistent actions compound over time, creating significant results

The beauty of this approach is that once these habits, systems, and processes are firmly established, you spend less time and mental energy thinking about money management while achieving better results. It's like setting your financial life on autopilot. Not because you're disengaged, but because you've programmed the right course.

Consistent Financial Behavior Eventually Creates Wealth

True wealth doesn't come from get-rich-quick schemes or financial shortcuts. It grows naturally from the soil of consistent financial behaviors that you maintain year after year, month after month, day after day. You have to become CONSISTENT at a thing before you can become exceptional at that thing.

When you understand that wealth is simply what happens when you do the right things with your money over time, it completely changes how you approach building wealth in these ways:

- Instead of looking for shortcuts, you focus on consistency

- Instead of making dramatic changes, you make sustainable ones

- Instead of measuring progress in days or weeks, you think in years and decades

- Instead of comparing yourself to others, you focus on your own financial journey

When you understand that wealth comes from behavior over time, patience becomes easier. You don't expect overnight results, just as a farmer doesn't expect to harvest the day after planting. You trust the process, knowing that consistent application of sound financial principles will eventually produce the results you seek.

This long-term perspective also helps you weather the inevitable financial setbacks that everyone experiences. A job loss, medical expense, or economic downturn might temporarily disrupt your progress, but it doesn't derail your journey because your focus isn't on short-term gains but on lifetime financial behaviors.

How Non-Negotiable Financial Standards Create Success

When we talk about carving your money management habits in stone, we're talking about making them non-negotiable parts of your life—practices you maintain regardless of circumstances.

This level of commitment means:

- You don't skip your monthly budget when you're busy

- You don't raid your emergency fund for non-emergencies

- You don't take on bad debt when you see something you want

- You don't abandon your savings plan when something more entertaining comes along

Making these behaviors non-negotiable doesn't mean you never adjust your approach. Your specific budget categories will change as your life circumstances evolve. Your emergency fund target might increase as your family grows. Your investment strategy might shift as you approach retirement. But the fundamental principles remain constant—you're always managing your money intentionally, living below your means, avoiding bad debt, and maintaining financial security.

Financial Success Requires Commitment to Permanent Lifestyle Change

The difference between temporary financial improvement and lasting wealth comes down to your commitment to permanent change. This isn't about motivation, which comes and goes. It's about dedication to a new financial identity.

Consider making these commitments explicit:

- **Regular financial reviews**: Commit to reviewing your budget, savings, and investments on a consistent schedule (monthly, quarterly, and annually).

- **Accountability partnerships**: Share your financial goals and progress with a trusted friend, family member, or financial advisor who can help keep you accountable.

- **Continuous learning**: Commit to ongoing financial education through books, courses, or mentorship to refine your approach as you grow.

- **Written financial principles**: Document your core financial beliefs and practices to refer back to when making significant financial decisions.

- **Celebration of milestones:** Acknowledge and celebrate your financial achievements to maintain motivation for the journey.

These commitments create structures that support your financial lifestyle even when life gets busy or challenges arise. They transform financial management from something you have to remember to do into something that's integrated into the rhythm of your life.

The reward for this commitment isn't just financial security. It's a profound sense of freedom that those without financial discipline rarely experience.

The Freedom of Financial Discipline

True financial freedom comes through discipline. When financial management becomes your lifestyle, you experience a level of freedom that those who live reactively with their money never know.

This freedom appears in multiple ways:

- **Freedom from financial anxiety:** You sleep better knowing you have systems in place to handle life's uncertainties.

- **Freedom from financial emergencies:** What would be emergencies for others become manageable situations for you.

- **Freedom to pursue opportunities:** With your financial foundation secure, you can say yes to opportunities that align with your goals.

- **Freedom to be generous:** Financial stability allows you to share your resources with others from a position of strength.

- **Freedom to make life changes:** Whether it's changing careers, relocating, or starting a business, financial discipline gives you options others don't have.

This is the ultimate paradox of financial discipline as a lifestyle: The boundaries you set around your money actually expand your life options rather than restricting them. The temporary sacrifices you make create lasting freedom that those who spend without limits never experience.

As you enjoy this freedom and continue your financial journey, you'll encounter a new challenge: adapting your management approach to match your growing resources and evolving goals.

You Have to Manage at a New Level to Get to a New Level

As you incorporate these financial principles into your lifestyle, you'll find yourself achieving levels of financial stability and growth you might once have thought impossible. But the practices that got you to your current level may not be sufficient to reach the next one.

As your wealth grows, your management approach needs to evolve accordingly. The budgeting system that worked perfectly for a $50,000 income might need refinement when you're earning $100,000. The investment strategy that built your first $100,000 might need adjustment as you approach $1 million.

This doesn't mean abandoning the principles we've discussed, it means applying them at increasingly sophisticated levels as your financial situation develops. The core practices remain the same, but their specific implementation evolves.

This growth mindset ensures that your financial management lifestyle continues to serve you well regardless of how your circumstances change. Whether you experience significant income increases, inherit assets, or build substantial wealth through your efforts, the foundational practices adapted to your new reality will continue to protect and grow your resources.

Your Financial Journey Continues

We've covered the essential foundation of financial success—the management principles that must be in place before you can effectively build significant wealth. With these seven steps implemented as a lifestyle, you've positioned yourself for financial growth that many people never experience.

But this isn't the end of your financial journey, it's just the beginning of a new phase. With your foundation solidly in place, you're now ready to build upon it with investment strategies, real estate opportunities, business ventures, or whatever wealth-building approaches align with your goals and interests.

The beautiful thing about having completed your financial foundation is that you can pursue these wealth-building strategies from a position of strength rather than vulnerability. You're not gambling with money you can't afford to lose or taking risks out of desperation. You're making strategic decisions with resources you've carefully managed, protected by the safety nets you've established.

Financial management isn't just about the technical steps of budgeting, saving, and eliminating debt. It's about transforming your relationship with money so that it serves your goals rather than controlling your life. It's about creating a lifestyle of intentionality, discipline, and foresight that produces financial peace and freedom.

The habits you've developed through this process will serve you well for the rest of your life, creating opportunities and security that would otherwise be impossible. By making these principles a permanent part of your lifestyle, you've set yourself on a path to lasting financial success.

Your money is now your employee, and you are firmly established as the manager. Keep leading with confidence, discipline, and vision, and watch how your financial future unfolds in ways you might never have imagined.

Conclusion

Your Roadmap to Financial Freedom

Now that you know the 7-Step System to take control of your money and build lasting wealth, you have the blueprint for transforming your financial life. This isn't just theoretical. I've lived both the struggles and the triumphs of this journey.

My wife and I were in student loan debt until I was 51, watching our original $50,000 balloon to over $70,000 before finally paying it off in 2021. Those were decades of missed wealth-building opportunities I'll never get back. Don't make the same mistake.

Think about the foundation we've built together:

1. **Management** as the cornerstone of financial success

2. A **budgeting system** giving you control over your money

3. An **initial emergency fund** of $3,000—your financial seatbelt

4. A plan to eliminate **bad debt**—freeing you from financial chains

5. **Strong credit** as a strategic tool for acquiring appreciating assets

6. A **full emergency fund**—providing complete security

7. These practices as a **permanent lifestyle**—carved in stone

When I first saved my full emergency fund of $30,000, that feeling of security was indescribable. Suddenly, the constant background anxiety about "what if" scenarios disappeared. Decisions became about what was best for my future, not what was necessary for survival. This peace of mind is what awaits you when you complete your financial foundation.

Whatever you mismanage, you lose. Whatever you manage well, grows. This principle has guided my financial journey and transformed how I approach not just money, but every resource in my life.

The financial management habits you've established aren't just for the good times. They're even more valuable during difficult seasons. When challenges come—and they will—your foundation will determine whether you weather the storm or get swept away.

Remember that you have to manage at a new level to get to a new level. The practices that built your first $10,000 in savings need refinement to build $100,000 in investments. The principles remain the same, but their application becomes more sophisticated as your wealth grows.

Ready to take your next step?

Whether you want to master one step at a time, transform your entire financial system, or get one-on-one mentoring — it all starts here:

☞ SmartMoneyBro.com

Whichever path you choose—even if it's implementing these principles entirely on your own—the most important factor is consistent action. Wealth isn't a six-month event; it's the byproduct of your behavior over time. The knowledge in this book has the power to transform your financial future, but only if you apply it consistently.

Don't let this be just another book you read and forget. Let it be the turning point where you took control of your financial story and began managing your way to millions.

To your financial freedom,
Eric, (Smart Money Bro)

About the Author

Eric Bowie (Smart Money Bro) is a personal finance educator, YouTuber, and founder of *Smart Money Bro®*, a movement dedicated to helping everyday people make, save, and invest more money with purpose. After rebuilding his finances from negative net worth to millionaire status, Eric now teaches practical wealth-building principles that work in the real world — not just on paper.

Through courses, books, coaching, and content, *Smart Money Bro* helps people manage their way to financial freedom — one intentional step at a time.

With more than half a million YouTube subscribers, over 40 million views, and a growing online community, *Smart Money Bro* is known for his no-fluff approach to money management. As a self-made, modern-day voice for wealth building and financial discipline, his message is simple yet powerful: *"The best person to take care of the old you — is the young you."*